M000031928

Five Minutes

300 Seconds That Changed My Life

Jack Zimmerman

Austin Brothers Publishing

Five Minutes
300 Seconds that Changed My Life
Jack Zimmerman

Published by Austin Brothers Publishing, Fort Worth, Texas

www.abpbooks.com

Author's Website: www.JackZimmermanMN.com

ISBN: 978-1-7375807-2-0

Heart graphic: www.vecteezy.com

Printed in the United States of America
2021 -- First Edition

To my wife Megan
who was at my side every day in the hospital and through rehab.
She is my strength in many ways, often making up for what I lost.
I would not have made it without her.

To my sons, William and Benjamin Brett Zimmermn.
I want them to have my story forever as something to look back on when life is hard.

Finally, to my best friend Corporal Brett Land.
We served side-by-side in Afghanistan
and he was my hero,
the guy I would have followed through the Gates of Hell.
Although he didn't make it home from Afghanistan,
he will never be forgotten.

This story is about my service with the 101st Airborne Division in Afghanistan. The black heart pictured throughout the book represents that service and was the emblem we wore on the side of our helmets.

As you know, the Kandahar province was the home of the Taliban, and the fighting was intense. I lost several friends during my time there, friends who made a profound impact on my life.

I have also made many new friends since returning home, a different man than I was before going. The veterans who fought for our country are special people and it is my privilege to work with them every day.

I hope some of the things I learned from my service can make a difference in the lives of many others. That is the only reason I share my story.

WHAT PEOPLE SAY ABOUT JACK ZIMMERMAN...

We lost CPL Brett Land in October 2010. This ripped through 2nd Platoon – how could this happen to someone so fearless and indestructible? We still had seven months left in the deployment and morale was low. Jack played a pivotal role in getting us back to operating with tactical and technical proficiency. He did this just by being himself. Not only did Jack volunteer to do all the electrical work to get our new COP stood up, but he was always prepared to lay the wire. Didn't matter how hot it was, how intense the firefight the previous day was, how much he wanted to call home. Jack would put his kit on, sling his SAW across his chest, and bring his best to every mission, every time. Despite being a PFC, Jack was unquestionably a leader in the platoon. Soldiers looked up to him, and NCOs and I relied on him.

When Jack got hurt, many of us were not optimistic he would make it, myself included. I will never forget getting the update a couple hours later that he had held on during the MEDEVAC and was undergoing surgeries. As the days went on and the updates were increasingly positive, we all began to become confident he would make it after all. As the platoon received these updates, our strength and cohesion surged. We went on to close out the deployment with a series of Air Assault missions throughout Afghanistan

– Jack would have loved them. He was with us, though, we all knew that. Jack, thanks for what you did for 2nd Platoon, and thanks for what you stand for as an American.

Danny Henry
Jack's PL during those 300 seconds

As Jack takes us on his journey, his wisdom from past experiences and a path through all obstacles while finding joy in the little things in life is clear. He encourages us to reflect on our own hardships and gives us the tools he uses to maintain a positive attitude. We have all faced and will continue to face hardship and tragedy throughout our lives, but regardless of circumstance or hardship prevail. Like Jack said, "everyone's life is hard to them."

—Luke Weinandt
Veteran & entrepreneur

A few years ago, I got an opportunity to be an assistant coach with the Cleveland High School Boys Basketball Team. I knew most of the boys at least a little since I grew up in town and still live there. Jack Zimmerman was a part of that team. Watching Jack that season and learning more about the real qualities of the young man as an athlete, a teammate, and a human being with compassion for others was an experience that will remain in my heart forever.

My lasting memory of Jack will be something that happened in the middle of a tough playoff game. One of Jack's teeth was knocked out by an opponent driving towards the basket. Jack wasn't worried about his tooth. He was more worried about getting right back into the game because he knew the team needed him. That situation shows exactly the character exemplified by Jack Zimmerman.

That willingness to sacrifice for others would be shown again a few years later while serving his country. Perhaps the trait that best exemplifies what Jack Zimmerman means to me is his resilience in the face of adversity. He showed it in that basketball game and has continued to show it in much more difficult circumstances over the ensuing years. I'm proud to know Jack Zimmerman and glad to have been a part of his life. There are many great life lessons to be learned from a man of his character. Jack's service to his country is admirable, but perhaps his greatest contribution can be found in the lessons he is committed to teaching today's youth. Thanks Jack, for your service and ongoing mission in making America a better place.

—**Dave Cink**

Meeting Jack in 2011, after he was wounded, I had the great honor of pinning him with his purple heart. Seeing how far his life has come since then has been truly inspirational. Jack and Megan are perfect *examples that love, a strong work ethic, and a positive attitude not only will get you through any adversity, but you will thrive afterward. I am proud to know them.*

—John Kriesel

Normally, a life-changing event such as Jack's takes a toll on your heart and motivation, but it just increased his. Jacks is the type of soldier that belongs in a case with a sign on it saying, "in case of war, break glass."

—J Michael Monahan

Author's Website: www.JackZimmermanMN.com

Contents

Foreword

Have you ever had one of those encounters when you meet someone and you know immediately you're going to be friends? That's what happened to me when I met Jack Zimmerman seven months ago. To be honest, we've never been in the same room or met face-to-face, but we've spent hours talking and listening.

Jack was looking for someone to help tell his story. That's where I came in because that's what I do—help people tell their stories. Our friendship should not have happened because we are different in countless ways. He's in the early stages of raising two sons, and my three sons are grown with their own families. Jack loves car racing, and although I live within a few miles of a huge NASCAR track, I've only been to the races once, and I was bored out of my mind. Jack is young and energetic, always on the go, and I'm at the point in life where staying home in the evening is always my first choice. We've never discussed it, but I suspect our politics are also quite different.

However, the main similarity between us that cut through all our differences is that we both live every day with a similar view of the world—a view from about four feet above the ground. We both use a wheelchair.

Jack landed in his chair as a young man in the prime of life. Mine is the result of polio as an infant. As I listened to Jack's story and experiences, it felt like I was listening to my story. Not the wounded in Afghanistan part (I never had anything that traumatic happen), but the way he has learned to handle life without legs.

We share much in common. Like the way people stare when you come into a room or how nervous they get when you initiate a conversation. He has learned in less than a decade many of the lessons it took me years to grasp. Jack knows that obstacles are simply opportunities or challenges. He is aware that attitude is the key to success in almost every aspect of life.

In *Five Minutes: 300 Seconds that Changed My Life*, Jack tells the story of what happened in Afghanistan and the impact it had on everything and everybody in his world. But Jack's story is not a sad tragedy. It's a tale of victory, or as he would say, "becoming the best new version of me."

I didn't know the old version of Jack Zimmerman, but I'm certainly impressed with the current version. You will be as well as you read his story. As a bonus, you will learn how the lessons that guided him can help you become a better person.

Terry Austin

Five Minutes

FIVE minutes.

It doesn't seem like a long time, but it might be, depending on the circumstances. If you're a student cramming for a final exam, five minutes isn't long. If you're a kid waiting for your dad to come outside and play catch, it might seem like an eternity.

If you're rapidly losing blood and fighting for consciousness, five minutes seemed like an impossible amount of time. Lying in the back of a truck after getting off a MEDEVAC chopper, the surgeon looked at me and told me if I could stay awake for five more minutes, he promised me I would live. It was the most pivotal moment that day, perhaps even my entire life. Five minutes seemed like an unbearable amount of time.

IT was March 9, 2011, a little more than a decade ago. The air was cool as the sun came up. My day started in Guard Tower 3, looking out over COP (company outpost) in Afghanistan. The COP sat near a man-made mountain that was visible from miles around. It was obviously chosen for its strategic location. There wasn't a huge number of troops in the COP, maybe two platoons consisting of fewer than 100 guys. Our primary task was to patrol the area, find the enemy, push the Taliban out of the area, and make the area safe. Our days were typically long, so when I came down from the guard tower after being relieved, I knew there was still much to do before the day was over.

I carried my SAW (squad automatic weapon) and other gear, including night vision equipment, and returned to my bed. I always carried about 1,200 rounds with me, along with all the other stuff needed by a soldier. The area is super sandy, looking like what I envision as moon dust, and it's hard to keep from tracking it inside the tent. There are always a few guys sitting at the front door, smoking, joking, or eating. I walked past them, made a few jokes and some small talk before going to my bunk to drop off my stuff.

My bunkmate was asleep in the top bunk. It was always dark in the tent as someone was always sleeping because of the different schedules. The front of the tent was for platoon leaders and others of higher rank. That was also the area where plans were made, and assignments distributed each day. A giant whiteboard contained a "to do" list of who was doing what. I was assigned to go on patrol for the day.

Two teams were designated to go out together, and it noted that Z-man, my nickname, was assigned to carry the litter, which consisted of a three-foot cylinder that contained the fold-out stretcher used for carrying the wounded. I took notes in my notebook of the assignment and returned to my bunk for a quick nap.

About a half-hour later, someone came by and hit me, saying, "Hey, we're going to a briefing for the patrol."

—PLATOON

Outside, we noticed everyone going on patrol was reviewing assignments and a map of the area. We would be northeast of Ahmad Khan; we called it "AK" for short. It was in the Arghandab River Valley.

Weeks earlier, when we first arrived at this place, all the stuff was still packed in the Conex box used for delivery, so nothing was set up. Our first task was to deploy the tents and get everything inflated and up and running. I was an electrician before joining the Army, so my skills came in handy, which meant I was heavily involved in setting up the entire COP. We were now living at Ahmad Khan, a place surrounded by opium and marijuana fields as far as you could see.

One of the crazy things about our location is that it was near the largest Taliban graveyard. We would go on patrol and kill a Taliban. Within a few days, we could observe the funeral just a quarter of a mile away in the cemetery for those we killed.

Our patrol set out to scout a teardrop-shaped area consisting of several villages. Our COP was at the base of the teardrop, so we headed north. We came to a large spread of villages but understand, when I use the term "village," I'm describing a maze of buildings where people live. They are all connected, but it doesn't make any sense. Walls are everywhere, six or eight feet high. They are not stand-alone houses like you would find in a U.S. community.

The walls were constructed with bricks. Each brick was hand-made from mud, straw, and cow chips. They were stacked and hardened. Seperate buildings, called grape huts, had holes were placed at intervals in the wall, and these were used to hang grapevines. These huts had a roof to keep the rain from the grapes. The walls were so compacted and solid that it was impossible to tell the wall had been shot up after a gunfight. They provided great protection for the Taliban as they used them for cover, firing their weapons through openings.

We pushed our way north and east and came to a large spread of villages. Taliban were active in this area, so confrontation with enemy forces was expected whenever we went on patrol. Upon arriving in Afghanistan, survival depends on emotionally adapting to these circumstances. You learn to live with the knowledge that something devastating can happen at any moment, but you still must function normally and carry on daily routines. This particular patrol fit that pattern.

We knew something was going on because we saw a large group of guys going in and out of the area surrounding the village. We assumed they had a cache of weapons and ammo, so our job was to find and destroy the cache. We anticipated a fight as we prepared to head out on patrol.

All of us had our gear near the ECP (Entrance Control Point) as we got in formation and set out on the mission. My team was on point, Sergeant Hurley in the front and I was on the right flank. Picture this like a flock of geese. Two riflemen were with us that day on the other

flank and behind all of us was the platoon leader. Our
First Sergeant was with us, and the gun team was behind, along with the interpreters as well as another entire team.

It was
late in the
m o r n i n g
when   we
pushed out,
encounter-
ing villages
where   we
had   been

—COP AK

several times before. We had become friends with one of
the elders, so we stopped and visited for a few minutes.
I remembered one guy because his son was always with
him, but he was not around this day. Part of the job was
to get to know the locals; they could be friends or ene-
mies; it was hard to tell. As the Saw Gunner, I stayed on
the perimeter, interacting with the locals to a small extent. It was an incredibly hostile area, and even talking
to friendly locals required being alert.

We tried to keep everyone at a distance because of
the fear of suicide bombers or vehicle borne IEDs (Im-
provised Explosive Devices) like a motorcycle or car. We

continued north, taking our time. It was spring, so there wasn't any vegetation, which meant no cover or concealment anywhere. That meant we could see any potential trap. The rainy season had recently ended, so we were walking across bare plowed fields.

We continued working our way toward the top of the village. There was a large berm on the north end, and I remember running up to the top and looking down into the town. I immediately saw two guys running. I hollered to Sergeant Hurley, "Hey, we got two guys running to town."

From my experience, I knew those guys were up to no good and were likely the guys we were looking for. As soon as I called out, I looked down and realized I was standing on top of an IED. Spotting an IED was not unusual. Often, they were nothing more than an old shell casing or dirty plastic jug filled with fuel, topped with nails and screws. When exploded, the nails and screws were propelled, seeking flesh.

It was obvious; the two guys were putting in IEDs before I saw them running. I scurried down the berm to watch the building the guys entered. The Sergeant put a charge on the IED to blow it up as I kept watching the buildings. The gun team was ninety degrees to my right and set up on a wall that looked toward the building; we were in a horseshoe shape around the building.

As soon as Sergeant Hurley detonated the IED, they began shooting at us, apparently thinking we were shooting at them. The gunfight was on. I had one guy pinned in the doorway as the gun team was throwing rounds into the buildings. As we were fighting, suddenly I realized that somebody got around us. We were taking rounds from the side, and a guy worked his way around through the ditch.

I remember returning fire on him and staying engaged back and forth while the others continued firing into the building. At that moment, the Kiowa helicopters arrived, throwing Hellfires into the buildings, and the gunfire wrapped up quickly. When it was over, we took a few minutes for a smoke and to regroup before heading back to the COP. The plan was to resupply ammo and water and come back to find the cache.

Leaving, we were in reverse order movement, so I was now in the back of the formation on the left flank, still as the SAW Gunner. We followed the ditch out of the village, walking north. The enemy was close so we jumped across the ditch. Since I was in the back, I was the last to cross. I was walking in my buddy's footsteps in front of me, step by step. The field was open as far as you could see, and it was huge.

We were skirting the village and knew the enemy was close. Weeks earlier, we located IED making material, so we knew it was a hotspot.

The Sergeant said, "Hey Jackie boy, they're going to hit us again."

"Where do you think they're gonna hit us from," I replied.

He said, "I don't know, Jackie boy."

We had an interpreter with us listening in on the radios and he could hear the chatter. He could hear that we were going to get attacked again so he told the Lieutenant.

I didn't have time to laugh or respond. I remember feeling like I just took off, blasted like a rocket. It felt like a really bad, horrible dream, feeling your never going to wake up, the kind when you wake up feeling clammy with sweaty palms. Only this time, I couldn't wake up. It felt like I was falling forever. At the same time, I had the sensation of 10,000 miniature fingers running up my back, like a flashy heat of 10,000 skin pricks. I remember tumbling and tumbling and tumbling like it was never going to end.

I remember thinking to myself and trying to figure out what the hell was going on. I didn't know if I was hit by Afghan army soldiers, an RPG, or what. I didn't know. I do remember landing on my left black flank, and my shoulder or neck hit the ground. It recalled an experience as a kid, falling on a playground from high up and landing on my back.

It was totally silent because I couldn't hear anything. I looked around to figure out what was going on, but I was disoriented. As I surveyed things, I noticed my left arm. My shirt's entire sleeve was blown off, and the backside of my arm was completely gone. That's when I knew I needed a tourniquet. I knew I had to tie off my left arm to stop the bleeding.

It was the only injury I noticed at the time, so I tried to get my first-aid kit. It was on my left side toward my back. I always carried it on that side in case I was ever shot. I could continue to shoot with my right hand and perform first aid with my left. However, my left shoulder popped when I landed, and I couldn't reach my arm back far enough to retrieve anything from the first-aid kit.

By this time, a lot of blood ran out of my arm, and I knew a tourniquet was vital. I knew there was one in my night vision pouch in my right-side gear. I grabbed that pouch, and it was at that moment that I noticed the smallest piece of skin, three-quarters of the way up my forearm

was the only thing keeping my arm from falling off. I picked up my arm, and every time my heartbeat, I could see blood gush

—JACK AND BEST FRIEND THAT WAS KILLED

from the backside of my arm. At that point, it dawned on me that I was in trouble.

Tracer rounds filled the air above my head as my hearing gradually returned. Faint sounds of gunfire were the first thing I heard, but I didn't have my SAW. With each passing second, it became more and more obvious I was in a really bad situation. It took some time for me to realize I had stepped on an IED.

At this point, I had no idea my legs were hurt. I was sitting in a crater, and my guts hurt so bad, like I had been smacked in the balls with a baseball bat. Reeling from the pain, I curled up, trying to find some comfort.

Suddenly, my buddy Daniels slid in on top of me and began working on me. He opened both of our first-aid kits and put a tourniquet on both my arms. I tried to stay low since we were in a crater, engaged with the enemy in a firefight. If I had seen all my injuries the way he did, I might have been tempted to give up, but he kept repeating, "You're gonna be all right."

Still unable to feel everything, I responded, "Hey man, you got to get off me, you know, you're pinching my boys."

It felt like he was kneeling on my nuts as he worked on me. The next thing I knew, Doc slid into the hole and immediately went to work. Doc and I were close friends, and he was frantic as he threw his bag down. Doc was from Wisconsin, and since I came from Minnesota, we felt like neighbors, and he was like my "number two."

When he got my gear off, I tried to sit up, thinking I would move to cover. At that point, I realized my right leg had been completely torn off. Within a matter of seconds, I saw that my left leg was also in bad shape. It looked like one of those Halloween decorations where all you see is the bones with my boot dangling at the end. My first thought was about the possibility of hopping on one leg to get to a better spot. I could see how many guys were occupied with me and became frightened about the situation.

It's impossible to describe what was going through my mind. There was a measure of fear of being hit again since we were in the middle of a live firefight, bullets whizzing around. The pain from my catastrophic wounds was beginning to set in, and as my hearing returned, the noise was deafening. All of that was clouded by my desire to avoid being a burden on my team. I didn't want more guys taken away from the fight because of my injuries.

It was obvious that I had to let someone else take over. They talked to me about what to do, even bringing up trivial subjects to get my mind off the situation. Daniels and I planned to get a house together when we got home, and he brought that up. He reminded me I would bring my girlfriend down and other stuff we had anticipated as if it were still going to happen.

I was getting tired, so, so tired. Everyone was talking and working hard on me. My right leg was torn off almost to the groin, and Doc struggled to find the artery to tie it off. He was finally able to grab it, and it hurt so bad. I was being overtaken by exhaustion, and it was a struggle to remain conscious. I remember looking up at the sun beaming into my eyes, thinking this is the place where I'm going to die.

The guys kept talking to me, trying to keep me going. I insisted that I couldn't talk anymore; I didn't have the energy. The thirst was almost unbearable; I was ready to kill someone for a drink. Doc gave me some water on a piece of gauze that he stuck in the corner of my mouth. It was surprisingly satisfying. Thinking I was at the end of my life, that tiny bit of moisture on my lips felt good.

My method for staying alive was to keep telling myself "Left, right, left, right," as I rolled my head back and forth. It was a way to focus on something I could do that required conscious effort. However, that soon stopped working, and I told the guys, "I think this is it."

Something happened at that moment—I could feel myself. It was almost euphoric, incredibly peaceful. The pain was gone; it was surreal. I think it was shock more than anything, but I was at peace with living or dying at that point. I was able to turn my power to something greater than myself, if that makes sense.

My right leg was completely gone; my left leg was barely there. I was waiting on the battlefield, rapidly bleeding out, with not much to hang on to. I was conscious enough to hear the "woof, woof, woof" of chopper blades approaching. I refused to be that guy who dies the moment the helicopter arrives. These guys came to save my life; I can't give up. They are risking their own lives.

I was critically low on blood, and the guys flipped me up. Doc was jabbing the needle into my neck, trying to find a vein. Finally, he said, "Alright, we just got to go. We've got to get him on the chopper."

I remember being rolled over onto my left side and then rolled back onto the litter. I forgot to mention that even though I had been assigned to carry the litter, I had carried something for Daniels on patrol a few days earlier, so he carried the litter for me today. Otherwise, the litter would have been thrashed, and I might not have made it off the battlefield. They picked me up, and I had the feeling it was all over for me. I could see my left foot lying on my chest as they sprinted with me on the litter.

The bouncing on the litter was painful as they carried me to the chopper. As they slid me through the door, it was the absolute worst feeling I had the entire day. I looked up and saw Sergeant Hurley already seated in the back of the chopper, and I didn't know if he was alive or dead. He was hunched over as the flight medic and Doc were talking.

The flight medic said, "I don't give a shit; we got to go."

Doc was trying to tell him what he had done, but the medic didn't care. We were still in the middle of a gunfight, and he wanted to get off the ground. I learned later that when the IED under me blew up, a big chunk of steel flew up and bounced off Sergeant Hurley's shoulder, hit him in the head, and knocked him goofy.

With an incredible concussion, he looked at me and said, "Hey, man, you're in tough shape."

I didn't sense a lot of confidence in his voice, and I felt like I was dying.

The flight medic looked at me and said, "This is going to hurt," as he punched a fast one right into my sternum.

It was a huge needle, something like a ten gauge, to feed fluids into me as fast as possible. It felt so damn bad but hooking me up to the IV and squeezing it into me made me feel alive. I watched him squeeze the bag right into me, and it felt so good.

He asked who the President was, but the funniest was when he asked what day it was. I responded by saying, "Does anybody really know what day it is in Afghanistan?"

I remember the chopper landing at the airfield and lying there while the rotors shut down. It was almost like I had a minute to reflect on the situation and what was happening. I thought I had been through the most chaotic part of my day.

As the noise of the blades grew silent, the helicopter door was ripped open, and that's when the chaos started. They pulled me out of the helicopter and threw me into the back of an F-350 type truck, a makeshift Army ambulance. We were at the Kandahar Airfield. The surgeon was in the back of the truck on my right side, and the anesthesiologist was on my left. The anesthesiologist asked if I was allergic to anything, and I immediately said penicillin—it gives me hives. His expression indicated that was not what he was talking about.

At that moment, the surgeon looked me in the eye and said, "If you can stay awake for five more minutes, I promise you will live."

He promised me life, and that was truly the pivotal moment of the day! I need to hang on for five more minutes.

Recovery

I worked as hard as possible to stay awake for what seemed like an eternity. Finally, the surgeon leaned over me and said that my five minutes were up, and I could go to sleep. The last thing I remember hearing was the sound of the surgical saw whirring to life. It was the saw that would finish what the IED started, removing my leg completely.

Memories are unpredictable things. On occasion, they appear for no reason, and at other times they stay locked away. A few memories are like getting Super Glue on your skin; they don't go away. I have one of those memories of that day. Feeling like I had been kicked in the gut, I told those around me that I couldn't stay conscious any longer.

It was not a feeling of panic but a sense of resignation—this is it. It was important to encourage them to tell my family that I loved them, and I began to see my entire life flash before my eyes. It was not necessarily a feeling that I was going to die. Instead, it was the overwhelming sense that I was going to be ok, wether I lived or died. A sense of God came over me. What I saw there is what I take with me.

I have a vague memory from the hospital. The walls were bare except for an occasional hanging medical device. The light was almost bright enough to drown out the constant noise of the machines. I felt like I was choking with the ventilator in my mouth and wanted someone to remove it. Although I was not sure where I was, it was obvious it was not a good place. I remember seeing a nurse leave the room through a doorway. Later, she told me that she ran out of the room to tell my family I was waking up. She moved away quickly, and I passed out again; I don't know for how long.

My next recollection of waking up I was surrounded by my family, this time the ventilator had been removed. Although the hospital room didn't look like anything I had seen in the past few months, my first thought was how all these people got to Afghanistan? Don't they know how dangerous it is here? I had no idea that I had been moved.

When I woke the third time, the nurse said, "Jack, stay awake."

As I kept my eyes open, with beeping machines in the background, she continued to talk, trying to keep me alert. I could hear, but it was like a dream. I felt like I wanted to move, yet it seemed my body was imprinted on the bed. She informed me that I was in San Antonio, Texas.

Then she asked, "Do you know why you're here?"

The memories began to show up. Vague recollections of the helicopter were the strongest. I made the leap to assume I had survived and was now waking up in the hospital. For some reason, they brought me to San Antonio.

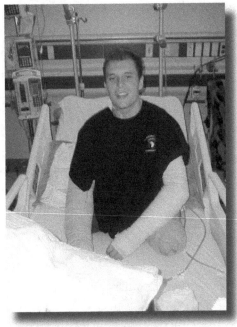

—JACK IN HOSPITAL

I remember thinking, "How the hell did I get here?"

Other memories slowly appeared—out on patrol, a gunfight, walking across a field, stepping on an IED, being slide into the helicopter. I even remembered the operating room.

So, now I'm here, they must have moved me here. The nurse was in the background, talking all this time, but it was like one of those Snoopy cartoons where all you hear is, "womp, womp, womp." I wasn't paying attention. All my effort was used to processing how I got here.

At the foot of the bed, I saw my dad standing. I heard him say, "Do you understand? Jack, do you know what we're saying?"

I knew enough to wonder why I was stuck in this damn hospital, and I knew I was all torn up, but I had no understanding of the seriousness of my situation. Oblivious to the seriousness of my condition, I thought, "What do I have to do to get out of here?"

Everyone gave an enormous sigh of relief, "He's awake!"

Dad was happy, but I could tell he was sad for me. At that time, he was much more aware of my condition than me. It hadn't been long ago that I was home, and Dad got to see me walk, not expecting that would ever change, but he was elated that I was there and alive.

Megan, my fiancé, was standing there, and I was shocked to see her. I was surprised she was there because I don't think we had ever talked about this happening. I had just proposed to her on my recent two-week break at home, but neither of us expected this to be our next meeting.

My Mom and brother were there, all standing around the bed. They talked about all the people back home and how everyone was concerned. The whole afternoon was overwhelming. So much to process.

The tiredness took over, and I passed out again, exhausted. It was comforting to have them all with me, but it was so much to think about. I still had no idea of the seriousness of my condition or how it would go in the future. It was time to create the best new version of me and what that looks like. We had to put me back together.

Both of my legs were completely gone, left on the battlefield in Afghanistan. My right was nothing more than a short stump, and the other was amputated above the knee. Both of my arms were also injured, and my right hand was seriously deformed. Most of my wounds remained open to allow them to be washed out frequently and prevent infection. Mud, dirt, and debris were packed in the wounds along with shrapnel, which required constant cleaning. Doctors were still in the process of putting me back together. I was taken to San Antonio because it was where I could get the best care.

One of the first things I discovered was they had put me in a medically induced coma for six or seven days. It was during that time I was transferred from

Afghanistan to central Texas. I was in the "Soldier Recovery Unit" of Brook Army Medical Center at Fort Sam Houston. My "tour of duty" in the hospital lasted eight weeks and encompassed more than 20 surgeries. Two of the weeks were in the Intensive Care Unit (ICU).

I was fortunate. Spending so much time on the battlefield, I watched many Taliban soldiers get injured, and they were often stuffed into the back of a car and drug off to whatever they used as a Medivac. I had a chopper with experienced medics fly me out of danger and take me to some of the finest medical facilities in the world. State-of-the-art machines and every other necessary device were available. Even infections that would be deadly to many soldiers were treatable. I received the kind of care that promised a future.

Just coming back to the States, where so many things were already in place, was huge for me. A few months earlier, I watched my best friend get killed by the very same thing I experienced. He wasn't able to leave the battlefield alive, not able to meet his daughter. My perspective from the beginning was to thank God that I'm still alive.

I can tell you that survivor's guilt is a thing, but I chose gratitude rather than guilt. I decided to be someone who is looking for solutions, not moaning about the loss of possibilities.

Each night I received a briefing for the treatment plans for the next day. Often it meant surgery, and they told me what they planned to do to put my body back together. One group worked on my legs, another on my right arm, and another on my left arm. They worked together to accomplish specific goals each day.

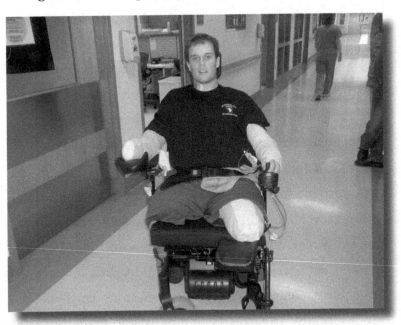

Much of it involved reconstructing my right arm. It had been shattered and needed to be reshaped. The doctor told me later the easiest approach would have been to take the scissors and, with a quick snip, cut it off and stitch it up. It's what we think of as being "old school" military. Doctors today think in terms of how to fix things. Give it the best shot to be useful.

They ended up putting a rod down my arm and reconstructing everything to it and covering it with my skin. The entire bottom side of my right arm is skin taken from my stomach, and the same is true for my left forearm. I went at least a month without seeing my right arm, other than an occasional x-ray or dressing change.

On my left leg, they took four more inches from the femur to clean up the amputation area to reduce the risk of infection and make it look better and more functional for prosthetics. There wasn't much leg to work with on my right side, only about four inches of the femur and little skin to cover the wound. It felt tight for a long time. I ended up having to get drains put in my legs to handle the drainage from infection caused by the shrapnel. One night, my fiancé completed giving me a bath, actually a sponge bath, washing my hair and everything, and then she thought I had wet the bed. It was embarrassing. My catheter had just been removed, and I was thinking, "What the heck is going on? My plumbing is not working," and I was freaking out.

She told me it was alright and not to panic, insisting that stuff like this must happen all the time. She rolled me around and put clean sheets on the bed. When she finished, she sat down, and as we talked, she realized the bed was soaked again. The fluid was yellow, and she noticed a spot where it was running out of my leg, out of an old stitch.

It turned out to be an infection, deep down in the tissue, sitting there growing without detection. There was no soreness or swelling. The next morning, they took me to emergency surgery and shoved tubes into all the pockets to allow them to drain. A lot of my stay in the hospital was dealing with this type of stuff that frequently popped up unexpectedly.

Numerous friends and family members were in my room often. My fiancé never left, sleeping with me every night. We had some of the best times watching shows at night on the computer. We were tied to the Ethernet cable since there was no Wi-Fi back then. She made sure I ate, which I was able to do very well. They wanted me to eat continually, and it went well with watching TV.

A day didn't pass without realizing how lucky I was with all these people who cared for me. My soon-to-be wife was amazing. She was young but kept everything organized. The amount of mail I had coming in became a joke on the floor. It was so much they used a cart to bring it to my room. Megan sat and opened the letters and read them to me. They came from all over the place, saying, "You don't know who I am, but I heard about you and just wanted to send a card."

In addition, many military Generals and other officials passed through the hospital to wish us well. While in Recovery one day after surgery, I was waiting, ready to return to my room, but nothing was happening. I didn't know why the delay. My blood pressure was good, heart rate fine, but I was stuck in Recovery. I was hungry; obviously, I was always hungry. Other than staring at a curtain, there was nothing to do.

I had been in the hospital nearly eight weeks by this time, so I knew the nurses. I singled one out and asked if I could leave to return to my room. All I could get from her was, "Not yet."

I eventually learned that the hospital was on lockdown. Hearing that, my mind immediately went into protect mode, thinking about my family upstairs in my room. The nurse told me no one was even allowed on the elevators. I sat there for two or three hours longer than I should have, and when I finally got back to my room, I was fuming mad.

I discovered my mom and others were happy and laughing it up. They said, "You're not gonna believe who was just here."

I didn't want to hear about it because I had been staring at a hospital curtain for several hours when I could have been watching March Madness; I was fuming mad. It turns out the First Lady and Second Lady were visiting the hospital to encourage the troops. I'm glad my mom, Megan, and a few others got to be there, but I still gave them a hard time for leaving me waiting in recovery.

Among the visitors were some friends from home. They rented a car for spring break and stopped by to see me for a couple of days, heading to South Padre Island. It was cool they took time out of their vacation to see me, which really cheered me up. Anything familiar and resembling normalcy was a welcome experience because I was at the point where it felt like nothing would ever be the same again.

Before leaving the hospital, I had to learn how to maneuver a shower. They had a place mocked up like an apartment. It was hard and brutal, but it was one of the boxes that had to be checked before leaving. At first, all my wounds were covered with plastic, which made it feel even more awkward. For three days before going down there, my therapist told me the first rule of taking a shower was that I had to sing a song.

We got down there, and that first shower felt amazing. It was like an accumulation of stuff that had been building on me was washed down the drain. Thinking about the next step of being able to leave the hospital, I broke into song, "Don't break my heart; my achy breaky heart."

Everyone died laughing; the therapist was surprised that I remembered. The experience felt like a huge win. Something as simple and mundane as a shower was a massive victory for me. It was a victory I needed. My recovery had a long way to go, and we were still on the first leg of the journey, no pun intended. But we were moving in the right direction.

During the spring and summer months, the news reports when a tornado touches down at some place, usually in the south. They often show video footage of the damage caused by the storm, and obviously, they pick the worst damage. The pictures are filled with scattered tree branches, building material, and mud to the extent that little is recognizable. We seldom see it on the news, but clean-up and construction crews sometimes show up and clear away the debris within a few days or hours.

At that point, you can see where houses once rested are nothing but flat, vacant lots. However, the foundation often remains intact. It's out there by itself, waiting for someone to rebuild the house. That image is how I felt during recovery. There wasn't much left of me. I left a huge chunk of me in Afghanistan. My family, my friends, and my attitude reminded me that the foundation was still there. All I needed to do was rebuild. If it was up to me to decide, I knew it was possible.

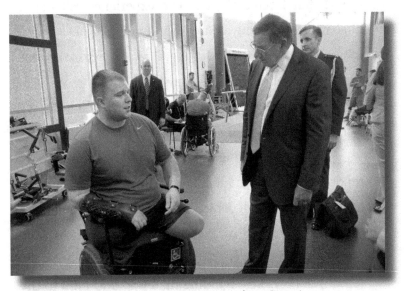

—JACK AT CFI (CENTER FOR INTREPID) IN SAN ANTONIO WITH SECRETARY OF DEFENSE LEON PANETTE

Define the Rest of
Your Life

As I gathered information about my situation, I was at a point where I had to make some hard choices and difficult decisions. It was time to look at what the rest of my life was going to be. At that moment, I decided I wasn't going to let an IED define my life. I took a one-eighty and refused to allow the Taliban to win by taking away my freedom and my life. I didn't want anyone to look at me and say, "There's the guy who stepped on an IED, and his life stopped."

I have hesitated for years to write this book because I didn't want to spend forever promoting a book and talking about one day for the rest of my life. I want to go out and do something else. I want to live. Getting blown up is at the beginning of the book because it is not the end of my story. There is still so much stuff to experience, and I was far from ready to live as if this was the last day of my life. I was not going to be bedridden. Besides, I'm not patient enough to wait in bed and die. I had a life to live, and I was going to do it.

At that point, I had no idea of what my life was going to look like. How long I was going to be in the hospital was only one of the countless questions on my mind. There were so many things I needed to learn. Honestly, I had to learn how to relive my life, starting with the most basic things people do every day from the point of waking up in the morning.

One thing people don't understand when you experience significant body alterations—your mind stays the same. I had the same mind but a different body. Now I had to figure out what that meant. There was nobody with an identical body who could teach me how to do things. They had similar injuries, but not identical. Every person is unique, and they must learn how to do things in their own unique way.

In a way, it's like a newborn baby. We've all watched as a baby learns something new. Parents get excited, often when they do something accidentally, but they keep trying and learn to do things intentionally. The baby pulls himself up, then learns to stand. After a short time, he lets go and stands on his own. Next thing you know, he takes a step, and then another.

Trial and error are how the body learns; except I had a tremendous advantage. I had an adult mind. Although I had to teach my body how to move in new ways, I knew what to do, which sped up the learning process.

That is how I learned how to do everything. I plugged away, day after day, trying different techniques and learning what works for me. After a short time, I realized my body was coming back together, piece by piece. It was time to figure out what the rest of my life was going to look like.

It was also apparent that everyone was looking at me, wondering what I was going to do. I might have been overly self-conscious, but it seemed like every move I made was noticed by each person in the room. Sometimes they would comment that I was doing well, but most of the time it felt like they weren't sure what to say or how to react. I felt a responsibility to help all the family members deal with my new situation.

The way I reacted to everything was crucial. My reactions determined how everything ended up and what happened for the rest of my life. I was aware that with a good attitude, I could overcome anything, and with a bad attitude, I couldn't overcome anything. I attacked everything with the positive attitude that I was going to figure it out and succeed. It was never a matter of "am I going to do that," but "how am I going to do it."

I amazed myself because I don't recall ever looking at anything as a problem. I saw it as something we had to get through, get beyond, or figure out how to make it work. Quickly, I discovered it didn't take more energy to have a good attitude and react positively. In fact, it required less energy because it made more people want to be around and work with me. It was a valuable lesson that applies to everyone—the way you react to a challenge matters to everyone in your life. I worked at never looking at something as a problem. Instead, I saw them as something we had to get through or beyond; to figure out how to make it work. There were so many different reasons why my reaction mattered. And I think that's true for all of us in our lives.

Waking up in ICU was more than simply opening my eyes and gaining consciousness. It was me waking up to a new reality. It was time to shape my attitude and build my perspective. This was frequently brought home to me with everything I tried.

I recall early in the recovery process, my Occupational Therapist said, "Jack, touch your nose!"

Who would have thought that I would have to learn to touch my nose, but he specified that it was my first goal in the process. I spent a few days in that hospital bed, trying to touch my nose. I thought it was ridiculous, but it was clearly not that easy. I was a 21-year-old guy spending my days trying to do nothing more than touch my nose. It was a daunting task because my elbow was shattered. My arm didn't work. My other arm was useless.

It was the beginning of rebuilding my body. I was at the point where every time I wanted a drink of water or a bite of food, someone had to be there to give it to me. However, once I could touch my nose, I could feed myself, reach my water glass, and even brush my teeth. I remember the therapist stretching my neck and pulling on my arm so it would bend enough to reach my nose. I worked on it by myself constantly.

Within a few days, I was able to touch my nose two or three times a day. Then I got to seven on the next day and then 242 on the third day. It kept getting easier and easier, faster and faster, more efficient. Practice and stretching, and persistence made it possible. Every part of my body faced the same challenges.

Sitting up in bed was nearly impossible. It was brutal not having any legs to provide balance. Legs also act as a counterweight for sitting up. I went from being one of the toughest infantrymen in the US Army to learning how to sit up in a bed. The first time was incredibly painful, and I struggled with how I would ever do this. I couldn't sit for more than a minute.

Being in the wheelchair was equally difficult. I removed the side of the wheelchair to practice getting in and out and then sitting up without leaning on the arm-rest, like sitting on the bed. I remember thinking this is going to be hell, a long process. My arms didn't work; I had no legs. Everything was shredded, but Megan helped me into the chair every day and would help me get positioned. They insisted she and I do it alone to prepare us for when we left the hospital. We took countless trips around the hospital and even went to the cafeteria to eat together. It was nice to get out of the room.

Everything in the hospital was difficult. One of the most difficult was the fact that Megan was my main caregiver. She did everything for me, never leaving my side the entire time. It was phenomenal to see her commitment and concern. She was my rock, and I knew I could always count on her. But the hard part was accepting that she had to do so much; I was of little help to her or even myself. At the time, the Army didn't recognize her because we weren't married. We made it clear, that the minute I got out of there, our goal was to get married.

She made all the preparations, putting all the paperwork together. I was about ready to get out of the hospital, and she and my brother went to the courthouse and got a marriage certificate. She tried to use a Power of Attorney to get the license the first time she went, but that didn't work. That's why my brother went with her, to sign on my behalf.

The next step was to find housing. It was difficult because numerous wounded vets showed up at the same time. The surge of the war sent them all to the hospital. All the places were full as they were not anticipating so many wounded.

A room opened, but I felt I was not ready to leave the hospital yet, but I really did want to get out of there. If it hadn't been for the infection, I would have been out two weeks earlier. But when the opportunity came up, we moved. We had a room, and I had a shower bench chair installed, and it was a process. You just don't know how everything is going to work. It takes time to experiment and figure out how to do things. It was a scary process, but I was finally out of the hospital.

Pain was a major problem. I mentioned earlier about the pain of sitting in my chair, but there was also pain in my what's left of my legs and back. Every part of me was sore for a long time. Even my stomach ached because of all the skin grafts. The front of my body was brown from the removed skin, the color of cheap meat.

I need to say that the medical people did a great job helping me deal with the pain. In the beginning, they put me on Lyrica, but I couldn't take the side effects. Being a young, fit infantryman, it was difficult, and between the medicine and lack of physical conditioning, the weight gain seemed to happen overnight. I don't take any meds now, but I can understand how so many people get addicted.

One of the first things I learned in the hospital is that phantom pains would be a problem I would deal with my entire life. When it comes on, I try to focus on something else but many times I not able to because it comes on so strong. It feels like I'm stepping on a nail, or the ball of my ankle being dragged on concrete. Even knowing what it is doesn't make it go away. It's something you just have to endure until it stops for some reason.

Recently, an episode lasted hours. It was some of the most exchuciating pain I've experienced. Six hours of that pain led my thoughts to get something to knock me out and sedate me somehow. Finally, I passed out from exhaustion. Waking up, my first thought was, "Thank God, that's over." After that, I slept hard for about 12 hours. It takes about four days for the lingering effects of a bad phantom pain episode to vanish.

Our apartment functioned well. Being young was a big help. I'm strong and can jump around, on, and off things. Managing a bathroom often presents the most

difficult challenges. Over the years, my arms have mus-
cled, and they compensate a lot for my legs. I never realized how important it is to having both legs and arms
and I'm grateful every day the doctors saved both my
arms.

Our place was located across the street from the
rehab center where I worked with an Occupational
Therapist and Physical Therapist. I was over there every
day, and it didn't take long before they began fitting me
for prosthetics.

Megan and I were married two weeks out of the
hospital, Memorial Day weekend. It was crazy weird,
like most of my life was going at that point. When most
people get married, it's a big production with photos and
special activities and events, and we missed all of that.
I still feel bad about it. We also missed out on a honeymoon, but we were so happy that we considered just
being together as our honeymoon.

I proposed to Megan the night before I was going
to the airport to return to Afghanistan. I asked her to
marry me and got on a plane. We never had the opportunity for engagement photos or announcements. We did
none of the things most normal people enjoy. My mom
and dad, and brother came down for the wedding, as did
Megan's parents. A couple of nurses came along with

Chaplain Goodson. We gathered at the Warrior Family support center for cake, fake champagne, and some food.

It would have been nice to have all that normal wedding stuff, but we didn't need it. We were certainly not disappointed. We were happy. We had each other, and I was alive. Being in a position to enjoy everything was a big deal for us.

I was now well into the process of defining the rest of my life. At this point, I knew that life would include an amazing wife and a body that was quickly learning how to compensate for all the losses. The rest of my life looked good.

—FAMILY BEFORE PURPLE HEART CEREMONY

Basic Training:
The Foundation

I left for Basic Training on the first of September in 2009. I got a ride to Sioux Falls to begin my military career. This was the first time in my life I had ever traveled on my own, so it was exciting. Even though everything was unknown to me, I was very excited. I had no idea what to expect or what anything would be like, but I knew it was something I wanted to do—no second thoughts.

I jumped on a plane for Atlanta, where I was to meet other recruits and make the trip to Fort Benning. They told me there was a big clock tower in the middle of the airport and everyone was to meet there at a specific time. I was early and had some time to kill, so I walked around the airport, searching for others who looked like me and headed to the same place.

About 15 minutes prior to the designated time, I picked up the pace to get back to the meeting place. I only saw two or three guys who looked like fresh recruits, doing the same thing, looking for like-kind. Finally, a voice rang out, calling for anyone who was supposed to be there at this time. It seemed like cockroaches coming out of everywhere. We were led down a long hallway, and as they called our name, we were checked off the list. We were told to get in alphabetical order and then loaded on busses for the trip to Fort Benning.

It was the middle of the night when we pulled up to our destination. As we came off the bus, they began screaming, welcoming us to Fort Benning and the Army. It was only a few minutes before they gave a short briefing and began shaving our heads. Next, we went downstairs and met a small woman who said, "You a big guy GI," and handed me a uniform saying, "this is the uniform you want."

Next was someone who measured our feet and gave out boots. They gave us everything we needed. At that point, we had everything we could possibly need to get started. We were then assigned a room with a bed and locker. They take everything you bring with you and lock it up.

We went to chow early in the morning for a week and then walked back where we couldn't do much since we weren't technically fully processed. There was a lot of standing around doing nothing. It felt like forever because there was nothing fun about it.

I knew nothing about the military. I should have researched more about what I was getting into. I just decided to go. I had talked with a few people, like the older brothers of some friends, and they would talk about a few things. One that I remembered was what they called a Shark Attack. That's when you get off the bus, and the drill sergeants go crazy on you, trying to freak you out. I kept telling myself, this is basic training; nobody's going to kill you. In my head, I knew they were only screaming at me to make me a better person, but it wasn't always easy to remember.

At first, it was difficult to get to know people. Everyone looked the same—identical uniforms, shaved heads. It was hard to recognize who you had spoken with earlier. It makes you feel like a stranger, with no comforts, no one around who cares about you, and all the screaming. It was incredibly overwhelming. For about three weeks, I felt beat up, wondering if it would ever get better.

There were about 30 in my Basic Training Platoon, and we were together from September until December. All we did was train. They would beat us up, break us down until we were exhausted. Every day was non-stop, from sunup until sundown, sometimes in the middle of the night, we were expected to pull fire guard. They worked hard to weed out the weak. The point was to discover who really wanted to be there.

We learned battlefield tactics, shooting, and all the infantry stuff. I must say, it was kind of fun, even learning how to march. The entire thing was one of the best experiences of my life, and I'll never forget it. I frequently recount stories of things that happened in Basic Training. I admit it was hard, and there were many times when I was homesick, longing for a meal my mom makes, but it was worth every minute.

It was necessary for learning how to deal with all the situations we would encounter on the battlefield. The main thing is that we had each other—no cell phones, no family. We all began feeling like we were alone, but we came out capable of doing what I would never have imagined. I was set on a trajectory to do things I'd never done before, things that pushed me to be successful in all of life.

I had never climbed up an obstacle course, walked on a beam high in the air, and countless other things I never thought I could do. I didn't have a choice. I just had to do it, and my peers were all around pushing me forward. I didn't want to be a failure in front of them. There were so many firsts, beginning with the Shark Attack the minute we stepped off the bus.

It has some similarities to playing high school sports, but not even close to the intensity. At Basic

Training, you don't simply build on your strengths; you're forced to work on everything, including weaknesses. It's valuable training for learning how to handle all of life. The people leading the training are the best.

Not only does Basic Training prepare you to be a better soldier and person, but it's also a place where you develop life-long friendships. When you go through so much together, it's only natural to learn to depend on one another, and that doesn't end when Basic is complete. That's one of the things that kept me going, even when it was hard.

At the forefront of my thinking was the confidence that I was doing this to defend my country, to make it a better place for everybody. My country had chosen me and allowed me to serve them. I didn't realize I was beginning something that would become the greatest honor of my life.

It all came down to the final few weeks. It was called our final field training exercise. They put us in the middle of the woods of Fort Benning, and we lived like infantry soldiers. We ran missions, walked formations, and suffered through test after test. It was the basics of everything we had learned.

Basic Training taught me much more than what I needed in Afghanistan. I learned far more than shooting a rifle, scouting an area, and surviving in the outdoors. Certainly, I didn't know it at the time, but Basic Training gave me what I needed to know to get my life back after stepping on an IED.

The following chapters explain lessons I learned in dealing with losing both my legs and having both arms injured seriously. I'm sure it was not the Army's primary intention, but not only did they prepare me for the Afghanistan battlefield, but also how to handle most of my life. I share them here to encourage many others who find themselves facing a similar physical challenge. More than that, these truths are valuable even if your challenge is not physical—the same principles apply to mental, emotional, social, and even relationship challenges. Wherever you are in life, I hope you can learn from the following pages.

The Best New Version of You

MORE than 60 years ago, Charles Dederich coined a phrase that all of us have heard numerous times. Dederich was a recovering alcoholic who worked to help others with alcohol addiction, and he came up with the encouraging phrase, "Today is the first day of the rest of your life." The implication was that we have the opportunity to reshape our life with the beginning of each new day.

Now that I was at the threshold of defining my life after Afghanistan, I intended to make it the best version of me possible. Whenever you set out to make yourself into something, it makes sense to make the best new version that you can. So, I took on the task of figuring out what my new self would look like.

By the way, this endeavor is available to anybody at any point in time in their life. You can look at your life, analyze it, and determine what you want to be. I tell this to people all the time. I was forced to do it because of the catastrophic changes in my body, but everyone needs to consider the possibility, especially when you struggle with where you are right now in life.

I had to learn how to rebuild everything in my life. I was faced with the reality that I would live the rest of my life from a wheelchair. I needed a plan for how my arms were going to work. The world would meet a brand new me, and I wanted to be the best possible version.

One of the first challenges was to learn how to use the available tools. Primarily, I mean prosthetics. The term describes artificial limbs. Technicians have become creative in developing new devices, and the VA has been on the cutting edge of using the latest devices with wounded vets. In my case, with both of my legs gone, it was only natural that I was fitted with two prosthetic legs.

My problem was compounded by the fact that both my legs were gone from above the knee. Using an artificial leg is much more complicated when there is no knee. With two knees missing, it essentially means using crutches for walking. I worked hard at making it work. The physical therapists were diligent and demanding. They didn't want me to leave the center without being able to walk.

However, I found it was too much of a problem to use crutches. Both of my arms and hands were tied up, and it was much more difficult to handle things or get around. Once I left the center, I ditched the prosthetics and used the wheelchair for everything. An incredible non-profit, *Segs 4 Vets*, provided an electric chair built on a *Segway* platform. I received the third model ever created as a tester. It allowed me to go everywhere with my arms free, even outdoors, across rugged terrain. The wheelchair is my constant companion.

How was I going to live in a wheelchair full time? From the hospital, we moved to a hotel that was off the post. This required numerous baby steps. I had to learn, for the first time, how to transfer from the chair into a car and then back the other way. Each new place presented new and different challenges. There is no need for a tragedy to be required to learn new things. It's necessary for everyone throughout life. Take small steps. Repeat over and over until you have it mastered. You might not be forced to learn new things, but it is necessary if you want to grow.

I figured out that my happiness didn't come from my legs. Neither was it dependent on my hands not being hurt. It was a process of learning what was important in life and what mattered to me. I was not only learning what was physically necessary for the new version of me but also mentally. I was striving to learn what the best new version of me was going to look like.

One of the biggest mental challenges was the change in my appearance. I had been six foot three inches tall and 240 pounds and in good shape. I was a military guy, walking around in a uniform, getting noticed, an impressive sight. When I entered a room, people observed. Now, when I enter a room, people still notice, but for an entirely different reason. The entire time I am in public, I sense everyone's eyes staring.

It wasn't easy to deal with in the beginning. I couldn't understand why everyone was looking because, in my mind, I was the same. It was like they saw something about me that I didn't see. It seemed like they were always studying, trying to figure something out. I had to learn to accept that it's fine for people to stare; they're curious. I've noticed it, especially with kids. They not only stare but often talk to you and ask difficult questions, while their parents cringe and tell them to be quiet.

I've concluded that people are looking because they can't imagine themselves being in my situation. They find it incomprehensible that they could go through what I've experienced. Many people have told me that they can't imagine going through what I did.

Most of us go through life without any idea of what life is about. We take so much for granted and assume everything is fine, and nothing significant will change. Any problem we ever have is far off in the future, so we ignore it for the moment.

I also quickly learned that physical changes could change relationships with people. For many, it changed the way they thought of me and ultimately how they related to me. My physical condition makes some people extremely uncomfortable. Sometimes they avoid talking about it, and others just avoid me altogether. Sometimes it's family that doesn't understand. They care so much and go into an over-protective mode, wanting to control decisions and telling me what needs to happen for the future.

Learning to be the best you, begins with understanding your limitations and what you can and can't do for yourself. Hear me carefully; I'm not suggesting you put limits on what you can do. That's the worst step you can take. I'm suggesting that you have a realistic understanding of what you can do physically and plan accordingly. Rather than limiting yourself because of physical inability, realize there are other ways to get things done that don't require certain physical movements.

Be creative and open to new ideas. Simply because you always did something a particular way doesn't mean it's the only way. You might need the help of another person, or perhaps you need to find or develop a tool. You can apply this to nearly any task. Perhaps the simplest would be to think about something you can no longer reach because you're in a wheelchair. Rather than doing without, think of a tool that will extend your reach. The point is not to limit yourself.

Another good example is driving a car. Obviously, I don't have feet to operate pedals on a car. That means I can't hop into your car and drive off, but it doesn't mean I can't drive. I drive all the time and have driven thousands of miles since being wounded. Just because I can't walk across a room doesn't mean I can't get to the other side. That's what I mean by planning according to my physical abilities. All of us can learn that truth. It's key in making yourself the best new version of yourself.

The day I was wounded, I had one of those experiences where my entire life flashed before me. It was like a super-high-speed replay of my greatest memories of the people I loved the most, not material things. I learned from the experience that all the stuff I had accumulated up to that point in my life didn't matter. My attitude about things changed. A crucial part of the best new you is the realization that materialistic things don't really matter, it's relationships.

As I said, my life and happiness didn't come from my strong legs. Instead, it came from the life I was able to live and the people I wanted to be around. I love my brothers and want to be around them. I wanted to live for my parents and now my wife and kids. These relationships are far more valuable than any material object, even our body.

My relationships extend to those who were overseas and dragged me off the battlefield. I want to be the best new version of me because there were more than a dozen guys on patrol with me that day who risked their lives to save mine. We were under heavy fire, and we definitely knew IEDs were scattered around; if I settle for less than my best, it will be a slap in the face to those guys who did so much to save me. If I don't do anything for the rest of my life, it cheapens the sacrifice they made for me. For what they gave me, I'm obligated to make something great out of my life.

The changes in my life were numerous. People saw me differently. The people I used to hang out with are no longer the ones I now hang with. It was apparent that I didn't have much in common with my high school friends when I returned from Afghanistan. I was attracted to the veteran community, where I discovered people who had the same experiences and knew me better. It's important to be around people who understand you as you struggle to make sense of the new you. If I successfully created the best me possible, I needed as many positive relationships as possible.

Coming home from combat is a sharp contrast. I had to reintegrate from military life to civilian life. They are like two different worlds. The community where I grew up was as unfamiliar as wearing someone else's shoes. I've always been a big community guy, supporting everything that came my way. I needed to find a way to make that happen once again.

I have found ways to make it work and be a part of the best new me. I'm very active in the local veterans organizations. I taught firearms safety, which led to starting a high school trapshooting team and still serve as head coach. I feel like I'm now a community leader, and people count on me. I like that feeling. I'm adding to the community in a positive way, and people need me. I never wanted people to see me in the chair; I wanted to be pushing the chair.

It took some time and a great deal of effort to get to this point. It was hard for me to be the guy who needed help, but my community reached out in an amazing way. I was the guy in the hospital who had his own mail cart because I received so much correspondence. Numerous fundraisers provided resources needed for my recovery; it was truly incredible how my community responded.

I'm so far in debt to these people, not financially but emotionally, that serving as a community leader is an exceedingly small way to repay them. I signed up voluntarily for the military. I was willing to sacrifice for this country. I didn't do it expecting them to take up the slack whenever I was hurt. But they did.

When I speak of my community, I don't confine it to the few thousand folks who live nearby. My community extends across this country, and I feel indebted to them as well. I've been in bad places, so I'm aware of how fortunate I am to be here in America. That's why I do my part. I'm trying to pay it forward, to do my part to make this an even greater place.

The more I give, the better I feel. That's how I discovered the best new version of me. I found it by going out and doing things for others. It's such a great feeling that I constantly strive to do more and more for people each day. Despite all the physical losses, I'm confident that I'm moving closer and closer to being a better version of myself.

It doesn't matter who you are, your condition, or your location; it is true that today is the first day of the rest of your life. Perhaps it's a decision we need to make each day – beginning right this moment where I am; I'm going to make this the first day of the best new version of me.

If It's In the Past, It's Broken

WHEN I left Afghanistan, everything about me was broken. It's hard to imagine a body more broken than mine was when they hoisted me onto that helicopter in the middle of a firefight. My legs were gone, my arms were shattered, my mind was groggy and fading in and out. Nothing about me worked; it was all broken. Consequently, I had to start a life for the present and future because everything in the past was gone.

I learned something through this experience that applies to all of us at different times. We all suffer from being broken. It might be a broken relationship, a job you can't find or don't like, a place where you're living that's inadequate, or even your family.

My first realization was that my legs weren't coming back. At first, I wanted to work on them, to fix them so I could use them again, but progress only happened after realizing they were broken for good. It would have been easy to spend time, perhaps years, dwelling on the fact that my legs were gone, but it would have been a waste of time and energy.

Instead, I began to shed stuff, peel away all the broken stuff and move on without it. Lying in the hospital bed, I could wish and hope that my legs would pop back on and begin to work, but at the end of the day, they didn't. I had to start looking forward and undertake how I was going to get myself healthy again.

I didn't focus on the things that were broken. I put my attention on the things I could do moving forward. My effort was directed toward finding a way to live a normal life. I can't walk, so how do I make a wheelchair work? I can't hold a pen in my right hand, so how do I use it in my left hand? Same with a spoon and fork, they didn't work in my right hand. It was necessary to relearn how to do everything, using a different method than before.

Success didn't come from focusing on the bad, the parts of me that didn't work any longer. I gave my attention to the parts of me that did work and how to use them to find a normal existence. Throughout my recovery, I had to keep my attitude positive. Every single day that I went to occupational therapy, I looked for new ways to do common activities. The first thing I do every morning is check my attitude because I have to jump into a wheelchair.

Since my right hand was not usable, I had to learn to use my left. They brought out what looked like Kindergarten books with large letters that I traced. It was hard and not a fun experience. Just a few weeks earlier, I was successfully completing some of the most difficult tasks on the battlefield, and now I'm sitting here learning how to write my name. But I couldn't focus on how bad it was, the broken things. I had to move forward.

I pushed through the hard things, one by one. Once I could do it, I worked to do it quicker and better until I could do it without thinking or effort, like before I was injured. I kept telling myself that if it's broken, it's in the past. If it's being worked on, it's in the future. I worked on things I wanted to be better, and most of all, I wanted to be independent as soon as possible.

I also wanted to go to school someday, so I needed to learn how to write. I had to learn how to transfer from the floor into my wheelchair in case I ever fell out of the chair, I could get back in. By the way, if you use a wheelchair long enough, you will fall out. Everything I did was aimed at finding the best new version of me possible.

I was in the perfect place for it to happen—a state-of-the-art building designed for maneuvering wheelchairs, surrounded by the best doctors and nurses for my injuries, and ideal rehab people to teach me everything

I needed to learn. If I had been a wounded Taliban soldier, I would not be alive. Even though a terrible thing happened to me, I was in the perfect place to deal with it.

The key is to keep a proper perspective always. With a good attitude, you can build on what you have every day. It seemed like every day I felt better, and stronger, and healthier. I knew I was going to get better and faster at doing things. When it came to writing, I had to work on nothing more than holding the marker the first day. It was a challenge to know how to use my left hand. Then I was able to move on to the next challenge, and by the third day, I was burning through a book of letters.

Building momentum is also important. Little victories turn into bigger victories if you don't stop and enjoy them too long. Keep moving forward. Whatever you're doing, try to get better and better and better, maintaining focus. Be willing to cut any anchors that hold you back and slow your progress.

One of the things I struggled with during rehab was concern over my buddies who were still in Afghanistan. They were still fighting, facing danger every day. One of my biggest fears was to look up one day and see one of those guys in the bed next to me. I did hear while in the hospital in San Antonio that one of my buddies was killed. It was a hard thing to accept.

It was not like having a high school friend join the Army and go off to war. You worry about them but not knowing what they are experiencing, it's hard to be too concerned. However, I knew exactly what was happening in Afghanistan and how dangerous it was every day. Although I cared deeply for each of them, I worked hard not to be sidetracked in my recovery. Once the momentum started, I kept it going because I was determined to leave all the broken stuff in the past.

A short time after I arrived in San Antonio, the doctor came in and checked everything each day. He would also explain what was happening and what to expect for the next few days, especially if surgery was coming up. He would always chat with me to see how I was doing and adjusting to my new situation when he came by. One day he spoke directly to Megan and Mom and Dad, asking if they could talk in the hallway. I thought it was kind of weird, especially so early in the process, only two or three weeks after being wounded.

My first thought was that he was telling them I was going to die. Why can't you say that in front of me? I couldn't think of anything else he would have to discuss with them. I told them to go ahead and talk with him, but deep down, I was concerned about what was going on. He pulled them into the hallway, and the main thing he did was express his worry that I was not grieving over the loss of my legs. He thought I should be angry or sad and all I wanted to do was ask when I could get out of here.

The doctor's concerns didn't change my family or how they related to me. I remember my dad told him that's just the way he is, that he's always been that kind of person. He was correct. I don't get hung up on stuff very often. I never allowed anything to get in my way. That's the way I approached this drastic change; let's get on with it.

The reason I have this perception is because I realized early in the process the reality of my situation. What happened, happened. I couldn't do anything about it so let's just move on. I was successful because I was able to put the broken part of me in the past.

Doesn't Matter How
We Got Here

THERE is a question many people ask when facing a tragic situation that is seldom more than a waste of time. There is no answer to this question and spending time striving for the answer accomplishes nothing. It is the question of why. Why did this happen?

The need to make sense of things drives us to find meaning in tragedy. We are convinced that if we know why something happened, we will have a better idea of what to do next. However, one of the reasons I have had success in dealing with my situation is that I didn't waste time determining how I got here. It's never really bothered me; I accepted what happened and my current situation and moved on. It is what it is.

I relied heavily on my faith in God throughout my life, and this experience was no exception. Understand that I'm not saying everything is fine or denying the reality of my situation. I don't have post-traumatic stress disorder, but many people think it will hit me one day, and I'm going to have a terrible experience. I can honestly say that I have moved on with my life, and as hard as it might be, it doesn't matter how I got here.

I never look at something and think, "If I just had my legs, this would be so much easier." I don't look at life that way. I'm realistic when it comes to any situation, and I'm well aware that I can do nothing to change it. It doesn't matter how I got myself into this mess; there is no sense in being mad and upset about something I can't change.

This is a big step toward making things work. I tell other vets frequently not to get sidetracked by what happened to them. Some suggest that I needed to grieve my loss for a longer period, but that's not me. I was sad, upset, and even angry, but not for long. Honestly, the key for me was rolling with my faith. I have prayed hard and tried to focus, not to get through and survive, but to become the best new version of me possible.

The way that I found the best new version of me was to keep moving forward. I was not distracted by continually returning to the past, trying to understand it better. When you find yourself in a difficult place, focus on where you're going, not what happened. Always be thinking about what's next, what is the next step? Keep moving.

While in Afghanistan, it was always the thing we needed to do. One of the best tactics during a battle is to keep moving. Don't allow the enemy to set up on you because once you stop, that's when he's going to attack. In my case, the enemy was the Taliban, but the enemy can also be procrastination, depression, or any circumstance we might experience.

For example, your enemy might be despair that you're not good enough. Many struggle with discouragement because they feel like they never measure up to expectations, either their own or other's. If that's your problem, keep moving. Continue to make progress, tackling new challenges, facing different challenges.

My injuries didn't just happen for no reason. I accept responsibility because I voluntarily joined the Army. When I signed the papers, I knew this was a possibility. There is nobody to blame and certainly no way to go back and redo it. The important thing now is to have a good attitude about my future. I can't imagine being inactive for the rest of my life because of this. There is still much for me to do.

Anger and bitterness are not options either. They are powerful emotions that sap strength from us and destroy our lives. Have you ever met a bitter person? The one thing I can tell you is that they are not happy. Resentment has destroyed their life. To choose that option would be like opting to stay in that hospital bed.

It was time to get on with life and become the best new version of me possible.

Make It Hard to Quit

STUCK in a hospital bed with the realization that all four of your limbs have been blown off is reason enough to give up. Family and friends were sitting around me, struggling with the same emotions. The easy and understandable approach would have been to give up. Nobody would have blamed me. After everything I had experienced, giving up would be expected by many.

It didn't happen.

Having all those people supporting and pushing me made giving up an impossibility. Also, I was not willing to allow the enemy to take me out. I just couldn't go there. There was no chance I would ever quit.

One of the biggest motivators was the memory of all my training and military experiences. I recalled the missions and the exhaustion we experienced on the battlefield. The training that carried us through these missions stayed with me. There was no way in hell I would ever quit because I had never quit anything in my life. I was not going to start at this point.

My only choice was to get better. Friends and family were at my side, supporting my efforts. It was clear they were willing to go through the whole thing with me. I couldn't quit on them. There were so many pushing me to get better, and I doubt they knew they were making an impact.

To get stronger and get a life, it was necessary to get my dignity back. I needed to be able to do the things I wanted to do. I had dreams; I just didn't know what they were yet. I was still young, and there were so many things I wanted to accomplish. With so much before me, I knew I would never give up. I also knew that none of it would be easy.

When you work hard to get things, they are more valuable because of the effort required. My goals increased in value, whether I was in occupational therapy, striving to touch my nose, or busy in physical therapy, pushing to get stronger and maneuver a wheelchair. I believed the result was worth the effort. Learning how to get in and out of a vehicle was a miserable experience. The first time I tried was hard, but not hard enough to make me quit. I was relearning how to do life.

In those situations, it's easy to throw a pity party for yourself. Some days, keeping motivated is really difficult. The key is to focus on the positives. It's a matter of staying positive. My hospital stay was different from many. I had such a bad infection that required being kept in isolation the entire time. It took a long time before I was able to see other guys, but eventually, the other guys who were wounded started coming around. They provided the inspiration I needed.

The guys provided information about what was going on outside as well as a personal perspective of what was involved with rehab and learning to walk with prosthetics. They explained how they were driving and doing all sorts of normal things. It was like being a kid again, hearing about what life could still be for me. I had a new desire to do all the things I thought I had lost.

Once a week, guys from the 101st First Airborne Division Association came by to visit. It was a bunch of old guys who served and had nothing better to do than come to visit us in the hospital. They always asked if we needed anything, and they would go get it for you. They were top-notch guys, and whenever they showed up, it brightened the day.

When I got out of the hospital, I began meeting with them and asked if I could tag along on their hospital visits. As we visited wounded guys, one thing I realized was being in the hospital meant they couldn't know what they were missing. I went around and took a bunch of pictures of places around San Antonio so they could see what everyone out of the hospital was experiencing.

This was before everyone had a camera phone, so they were elated to see the photos. I was like a window to the outside world.

My hope was to inspire them to work hard at getting out. I didn't want them to quit but instead see what they could enjoy once they were able. It helped me as much as them. All through my military experience, I wanted to fight for something bigger and better. At the end of the day, the one that you're really fighting for the most is your buddy to your left and right. Visiting the guys in the hospital allowed me to fight for those on my side. I felt like I was helping out, making it a little easier for them.

This attitude stayed with me after I got home. I helped to start Veterans Court and served three years as Commander of the local Legion Club and remain an active member. I stay involved in the veteran community. There are numerous resources available for vets after they come home. Much of my time now is spent helping vets access these resources.

Discovering the opportunity to help others, my fellow soldiers on my left and right, played a large part in keeping me from quitting. I was not just putting in the work for myself. I was doing it for all the others as well. A key to success in any endeavor in life is to give yourself to serving others. Once you make it about others, it is impossible to quit on yourself.

It's Not Easy, But It's Worth It

As I look back over time, I realize there were numerous things I had to experience to help me deal with my situation. In some way, my whole life was a build-up. It wasn't going to be easy, but it was certainly worth it. From the moment I decided to join the military, I was prepared.

It was something I wanted to do, which was reinforced by my entire basic training experience. One of the important lessons I learned was that you can't quit. There is no opportunity to quit. For everyone, there are times when you want to go back home, but I learned that quitting was not possible.

The temptations to give up can be subtle. It might be something as harmless as a phone call home or just tired of walking forever with no end in sight. But then you look at the guy in front of you, and he's not quitting, and the guy behind you seems tireless. All of those thoughts stayed with me in the hospital. It didn't make recovery easy, but it did make the hard work worth the effort. Seeing others fighting the same battle and not giving up is a great motivator.

I will always remember basic training and infantry school. On the final training exercise of Basic Training, when you walk what's called the "Stairway to Heaven," you realize the hard work is worth it.

Life is hard. Not just for me because I was wounded in Afghanistan. Life is hard for everybody. Despite appearances, everyone struggles with something. We all face a challenge that seems insurmountable. We use the phrase "born with a silver spoon" to describe a person born into riches and never had to work for anything. The truth is, even they have struggles. It may be an unhappy home, a difficult relationship, physical malady, or a myriad of other reasons. All of us have a mountain to climb.

Yet, many quit. We see it all the time. People turn to drugs and alcohol. Others just slosh through life, putting one foot in front of the other, hoping to survive day to day. An alarming number of people totally give up by committing suicide. The temptation to quit is strong, and the key to success is to realize it's worth the struggle.

In my situation, I could have given up in that hospital bed in San Antonio, fumbled my way through rehab, and settled for a life of loneliness and dependence on others. Instead, there was so much that I wanted out of life that I couldn't quit. All of it was hard work, and believe me, there were times I thought about quitting, but I continually reminded myself it was worth every-thing.

Now I have an amazing wife and two fantastic sons. The community worked together to provide us a home. I coach a high school trapshooting team, train hunting dogs, drive my own pickup, and have my own racing team, and even a book. None of this would have happened if I had quit. I was a young man missing both of my legs and had a useless right arm. Hunting, fishing, and sports had been my life, and it all appeared to be gone. I even had to learn how to be left-handed. But I didn't quit because I knew life still had much to offer.

It required 20 surgeries, painful, extensive reha-bilitation, and the support of family and friends, but I was able to get a life that was worth all the sacrifices. My story is not unique. Countless people have overcome insurmountable obstacles to experience success. One of the common characteristics of all of them is a refusal to give up.

The First Time is the Hardest

EARLIER, I described the difficulty of touching my nose for the first time. I can't describe how damn hard it was to move my arm so I could reach my nose. I spent hours pushing as hard as I could to get my hand to where it needed to be. It seemed like my finger would never stretch that far. Yet, it was crucial if I was ever going to eat or drink again without help. I stretched my arm and neck as far as possible to accomplish what most would consider a simple task.

And then it happened!

It felt monumental, but now I knew I could do it. Now I can do it a million times a day, and it's not hard at all. I don't even think about it. It's nothing like the first time.

I also remember the first time I got into a vehicle, the first time I went out in public in a wheelchair, the first time I met strangers. There were so many firsts. It was all a different experience for me. The first time I did anything was hard.

There are so many things in life that we're afraid to do or even try. It might be returning to school, changing careers, or moving to a new place. The first time you do it is always the hardest. What about the first time you got on a plane. Do you remember the apprehension? Can you recall how your senses responded to everything? You probably listened to the flight attendant give all the instructions and listened to every word from the pilot over the speakers. The muffled roar of the engines was a concern. You constantly looked out the window and when the first turbulence shook the plane, do you remember how scared you were? Every time you have boarded a plane since then has been easier.

The whole idea of making your way through the security hassle at the airport, getting on a plane, and landing in another city, seems like an insane experience until you do it the first time. By far, the hardest time. But it gets easier and easier every time we do it.

Often, we are so afraid of change, of being in an uncomfortable situation, that we stay stagnate. The tendency is not to do anything until forced. Things seem too hard, or perhaps even impossible.

Life is filled with firsts, but we don't remember most of them because they happened when we were children. We grow up experiencing first after first, but by the time we're old enough to remember, we've already done most things, and they're easy. However, as an adult, I was put in a situation with no legs and limited use of my arms, that I had to go through all that stuff again, for the first time.

The first time I had to shower, I needed to figure out how everything would work. All those daily activities that we take for granted are all new. Since I did not have all my limbs and abilities, learning new ways to do old things was required. I couldn't just step into the shower and turn on the water. The first time took planning and experimenting, and learning. In fact, the first time, the important part was not washing my body but determining the process.

Everything at that point in my life was the first time I did something. Many can relate to the fear of doing something for the first time. They know it's going to be the hardest, but after a few times, a process for accomplishing the task is developed. The most important thing is the realization that it's possible. Once you do it, you can do it a million times over, and you develop muscle memory—no need to even think about it. But you have to start from scratch.

Everything about how I moved around my world was different. I drove a vehicle differently. The way I pulled up to the dinner table was different. Every aspect of my life changed.

The realization that the first time is the hardest is a good motivator to keep trying. Success only happens when we don't give up. It would have been easy to give up on that first day trying to touch my nose. It felt like trying to do the impossible, and it was tempting to look for another way.

There was no other way. If I had given up after that first time, I would have needed help every time my nose itched or needed a drink of water. If I couldn't get my arms and hands to work, I would have missed out on the great life I have now. Even though the first time required every ounce of effort I possessed, once I experienced success, the world opened up for me.

I'm not saying that once you do something, it will be easy from then on. The second time might still be a struggle, but it will be easier than the first, primarily because you know it can be done. Don't give up too quickly on any of your dreams. Keep at it and build on any successes you have. It will get easier.

Control the Things
You Can

ONE of the craziest things we try to do at times
is change things we cannot change. We try to change
other people when they aren't what we want them to be
(ask anyone who has been married how that works out).
I learned early after I joined the Army that I was not
able to change policies and procedures. I had to go along
or suffer the consequences. Most of the time, I was just
going along for the ride.

I witnessed many soldiers dropping out because
they couldn't go along with things they couldn't change.
They were frustrated, and because they stopped trying,
they failed and washed out.

In Afghanistan, we thought we could change the
Afghan people's thinking. We helped them establish a
government, taught them about a better way of life, provided educational opportunities, and a taste of freedom
with the hope they would have a positive attitude toward
America. We had difficulty learning that once an American soldier has killed a person's father, teaching that
person to respect and support American efforts is very
difficult.

The truth is that we cannot change how we arrived at a certain place; it's in the past, we just have to deal with it now, in the present. In your life, things are going to happen that you can't control.

As I was nearing time to get out of the hospital, I was eager to get on with life. I had been in there for so long that I just had to get out. I didn't want to be in the hospital any longer. I got an infection I described earlier when my bed was soaked, and we thought the catheter leaked. Once they discovered the problem, I was rushed into surgery, where they drained my legs. I was devastated, thinking I was never going to leave the hospital.

However, I had to realize that this was something I couldn't control. A bad attitude is not going to help the current situation. I had come a long way already and draining my legs and another two weeks in the hospital was not the end of the world. When you're going through a hard time, it often seems like an eternity, and this problem will be with you forever. But, at the end of it all, it's just a short time in our lives.

I spent six weeks in the hospital. Looking back over 30 years of my life, that's a short time. The key is to fall back on the qualities we've built upon to this point in our life. Relationships, strengths, abilities, friends, family—these are the things that will carry us through. They will all still be there when we get through this trial.

It's like planning a big vacation. We get excited about the trip. Just as we are about to jump on the plane to leave for the resort, a big snowstorm hits, and we get delayed. There's nothing we can do about it. We can't control the weather or make the airline take us anyway. We can't change the situation. But we can keep a good attitude and make the best of what we have at the moment.

There are many things in our lives that we can't control, things that will happen to us unexpectedly, like stepping on an IED in Afghanistan. I can't control that, but now I have to deal with it. How I do that is what truly matters. We all face different adversities and challenges, and we have things going on in our lives we can't control. We can control our attitude; keep the right perspective.

Every time we have these experiences, we learn and grow. Sooner or later, when things come up, you don't look at them as devastating. You realize that everything in life is a complex problem-solving exercise, and we need to find the solution. Then we move in.

Here's the key. If you can control something, then take charge and make it happen in the best possible manner. At the same time, quickly recognize what you can't control and keep a positive attitude based on what you have already experienced and learned from previous uncontrollable events.

We All Have Adversity

PEOPLE take one look at me and know I've been through some adversity. When you see a guy with no legs getting around in a wheelchair, it's obvious he has faced some difficult challenges. I'm grateful for my life and being able to enjoy life as much as I do, but I'm aware there's nothing special about me.

Every person has adversity. For some of us, the challenges are obvious, like no legs. However, for most, the challenges are not so visible, and most likely, not even physical. When I look at my life and think about all the things I've been through, I try to remember I'm not unique. There are so many things that negatively impact life that all of us need to learn how to handle adversity.

We all have physical and mental adversities, and the key is to approach them with the right attitude and perspective that allows us to work through the challenge. Adversity is the first thing that hits me every morning when I wake up. I have to check my attitude because my wheelchair parked next to the bed is the first thing I see, and that hits me. I must overcome it immediately. It's going to be there. I can't control this thing in my life. But

I refuse to have a bad attitude about it because it will ruin the entire day.

There have been other things I had to work through, not all of them physical. One equally as hard as anything physical was losing my best friend in Afghanistan. That was one of the hardest days of my life. Numerous things bothered me from that day and caused anguish that I had to work through to overcome.

A flight of stairs is adversity to me. For some time, it seemed that everything was an impossible challenge. I couldn't go anywhere or do anything like before. It would have been easy to accept that and stay safe at home. Instead, I learned how to navigate things. Once again, I discovered that the first time is the hardest time. I look different than everybody else when I go out in public. Besides the wheelchair, I'm incredibly handsome! It seems that everyone is looking at me.

Most don't realize it, but people treat me differently because of the wheelchair. Some people are nervous about talking to me, and some even refuse to speak. Others talk slowly, as if I don't understand normal speech. People are nervous around me at first, and it's refreshing to meet someone occasionally who is unaffected by my situation.

Each person I meet presents a challenge, and I have to work through it. It's like complex problem-solving. As you do it over and over again, it becomes easier. You get to a point where things you thought were impossible a short time earlier, you're doing without a second thought. I've learned how to live my life and how to overcome these things. I found ways to make everything easier and deal with them emotionally. It is possible to overcome all these obstacles. A lot of things that we tend to label as adversity are nothing more than just life. Life can be hard.

The first step is to identify the problem. It's impossible to solve a problem until you know it's a problem. If it's a physical barrier, something like a few steps for me, the problem is readily apparent. The problem is, how do I get my wheelchair from here to there and get over these stairs? I can't control the reality that there are stairs between me and where I want to be. They are there, and I have to overcome them.

It wasn't that long ago that the presence of stairs didn't even enter my mind. If I came to them, I bounded up them like everyone else. Most people don't even think about steps. Many people have not even thought about the number of steps at the front door of their house because they are not a problem for them.

The next step is determining that you will not allow that problem to keep you from achieving your goal. If my goal is to get to where I want to go, I must decide I'm not allowing those few steps to stop me. It requires a decision ahead of time about how you will react when facing adversity. Those who wait until adversity comes to decide how to react are often the ones who give up. Success comes when we expect obstacles and also expect to overcome them.

This is key to making the best new version of you possible. Your adversity might be a need to get rid of something or someone in your life. It might be an anniversary that you're holding on to that drags you down, or a person who always brings discouragement, or a physical impairment like mine. It doesn't matter what it is or how you got in the situation. The important thing is how you are going to get through it. Knowing that you can and having the right attitude will allow you to do far more than you might think.

It's not going to be easy, but it will be worth it. You can't quit because when you do, adversity wins. Step out with the assurance that the first time will be the hardest, but it will get easier and easier each successive time. Each victory provides a building block for future successes.

It's the Little Things

WHEN I had the experience of my life flashing before my eyes, it was not what you might expect. I didn't see the major events of my life or the amazing sights I had seen. What was most prevalent was the relationships. I vividly remember my grandma sitting around a pool while on vacation and talking, and driving my car down Victory Dr. in my hometown while hitting all green lights. Little things.

The little things are what make life worth living. Stable relationships that are with us day in and day out. Everyday activities that provide comfort and security. These are the things that count. It's the small things that make life better.

I realized that it's important to acknowledge these things. The key is to keep catching these little windows that show up in our lives constantly. We need to focus on the things that go our way and not the big things that get in our way. If we're not careful, we get so blinded by life's major events that we forget the little things that make life what it is.

I have learned to appreciate and enjoy the little things. When my kids wake up in the morning, and
they're happy as they gather their stuff, it always feels
like a "win" to me, and I can build momentum off of that.
If they're grumpy and not ready, I'm not going to let
that tear me down, give me a bad attitude, and ruin my
day. There are so many little things that need to happen
during the day, so it's important to learn how to respond
to them.

Someone brings donuts into work today, and it
was unexpected—that's a "win." That's good, and you've
got to count these wins, and they add up over the day.
You catch a break or win the office pool, or your team
is victorious—these are all the little things of life. While
in Afghanistan, it was getting a Care Package. It sounds
so minimal to enjoy baby wipes, corn nuts, beef jerky,
and the other stuff people sent. But they made the day
brighter. It's like when you get a phone call from a friend
you haven't spoken to in a long time. These are what we
need our focus on, not the bad things that crop up.

It's these little things that often bring the most joy.
They can be the most meaningful part of our life. We get
pumped up about major happenings, and often our expectations are disappointing, but in the meantime, life is
moving on, and the little things continue every day.

In 2020 I attended the Final Four college basketball tournament in Minneapolis. The Championship Final was Virginia against Texas Tech, and it was an exciting game. I realized throughout the entire game that I was watching something incredible, perhaps the best basketball I will ever see in my entire life. Virginia had one of the best seasons in school history, and when the game was over, they were national champions.

I watched the kids who were frantically celebrating the victory. They cut down the nets and danced in the confetti. They were going crazy because they had put so much effort into making it to that point. All I could think to myself was, how can you guys be so happy right now?

I've been in competition and know what it feels like to win—I get that. They just won the championship, but their season was over. It's done right now. All the stuff you've built up for years is now finished. Other than one or two guys who might play in the NBA, their basketball career is over. They just won the NCAA Final Four championship, but the journey was over.

Looking back at all the games they had played, all the shots they missed, and all the things that didn't go their way—they weren't thinking about any of that at the end of this game. They were just ecstatic to win. As I thought about this, I realized they could achieve this goal because of the journey. When you stop and reflect, it is the journey that produces joy. All the things along the way add up. Games won, bus trips with friends, times in the locker room, wins and losses all added up to this one moment of joy as they cut down the net in celebration.

Someday you're going to be standing there looking back on your life or have one of those life flashing before your eyes experiences as I did. You might reflect on all the accomplishments in your life, but the things that will stick with you are not the "cutting down the net" moments but all the events and relationships that created those moments. For me, it's playing baseball with my friends, being at the racetrack with my dad, spending time with family.

The incredible life I've had is the journey. When I woke up in the hospital bed, it was like I was now living on borrowed time. I had a different outlook on life, one made up of all the small stories put together. I decided to appreciate the journey. To enjoy all the things I needed to experience to prepare me for the big challenges to come. Enjoy the day. If it's a day on the beach with your wife, realize this is the real stuff that makes life worth living.

It's the little things.

Every Day is a Chance to Impact Life

EVERY day on Earth is a journey, and as long as we are here, we have the opportunity to leave a mark. A good place to start is to realize that every day is a chance to impact a life.

As you've already noticed, I like sports, and I appreciate athletes. One of the great things about athletes is that they celebrate every victory. A football team doesn't wait until the end of the season to celebrate; they do so after every win. Even in baseball, with a 162-game season, teams celebrate together after every game won. They enjoy the entire season and appreciate each day. Most athletes are even fine after the losses because they appreciate the privilege of being a part of the contest.

The same is true with life. We don't have to wait until the end to celebrate. We have a funeral at the end of life, and everyone celebrates the person's life, but it would be a shame not to enjoy everything along the journey.

Enduring the trauma I experienced, and all the hard times, there were so many people who took moments out of their day to send me a letter or email message or do some other little thing that picked me up. It motivated me and made me feel like I couldn't let these people down. I came to realize these people were truly helping me. I had an overwhelming amount of support, and it impacted my life.

It was at that point I realized every day is a chance to impact a life, even if it might seem insignificant at the time. Even in Afghanistan, we did many good things for people. We helped them attain good, clean, running water or a new rug for the mosque. The people had very little, not even electricity, so they enjoyed simple things like pencils for the kids. I recall one boy who was happy as a peacock when he received a pencil, but he didn't have anything to write on. It was still his great possession and made his day. I began to realize how much we can impact someone's life with even the smallest gesture.

Other times it's big gestures. I never dreamed that my town would become one of my biggest supporters. They had fundraisers to support me. They helped build a home where it's easier to live. I'm aware I'll never be able to repay these people, but I can pay it forward to others. I feel like I have a lifetime of debt to repay everything that has been done for me.

If all of us worked harder to make someone's day a little brighter and more positive, imagine the impact it would have. It might be at school, at work, at church, at a restaurant, or even online; we come into contact with people constantly. Each contact is an opportunity.

During my time in Afghanistan, we got worn out and tired, but it seemed like someone was always willing to jump in and provide the extra help we needed. Working together made it easier for all of us.

There are so many different ways to impact a life. When I came home, I noticed kids in Afghanistan get wounded and it made me want to find a way to impact kids in my community and help them understand how fortunate they were. I saw it as an opportunity to teach firearms safety, a chance to make life better for these kids. Even with the kids in Afghanistan who had nothing and little hope for a future, there was still an opportunity to impact their lives positively.

People took time from their busy lives, including many from our community, and utilized their resources to make my life easier. I never saw it as them repaying me for my service. I always felt I was indebted to them for their incredible gift. Nobody owed me anything for what I had done. It's impossible to compensate people when they do something like this, so I decided to pay it forward and give to others. I have a lifetime full of paying it forward.

One of the most impactful people in my life was Jerry Bamberry. I met him while listening to a guy running for Congress. He invited me to sit at his table, and we talked. We moved away from the political candidate and discussed numerous other subjects by the end of our conversation. He suggested lunch. We hit it off quickly despite the fact that he was 40-50 years older than me.

He talked about some incredible experiences he had in life, and I was mesmerized. We became good friends, and he was like a mentor to me. He taught me about life. He was like a grandpa to my kids, and we spent a lot of time together. He coached me through life and was one of the most impactful people I ever knew.

He was very open about his own struggles in life, which encouraged me to open up and share. When I did, I felt better and found new resources for help. There was nothing official about our relationship, it just happened, but he taught me the power of being a mentor. It was difficult when he died because he had become so important in my life.

He demonstrated the power of overcoming a difficult situation with his home life and tough relationship with his father. He started out cleaning bathrooms at McDonald's. Eventually, he became an owner of a McDonald's franchise and was so successful that he was probably one of the wealthiest people in Mankato. But his money never mattered. I never took a dime from him. He was out there doing good for people, and I was the recipient of his goodness.

When you hang around people like this and learn from them, you're motivated to impact lives. It's important for me to live life to the fullest now and not give any days away. I can't afford to because so many people have given them to me. I need to be grateful to the individuals and my community. I'm grateful to everyone who impacted my life—my parents, teachers, coaches, friends, battle buddies, and all the veterans' help. They are the ones who shaped me. They sacrificed for me.

You have those people in your life as well. It's crucial that you not waste opportunities to pay it forward. Take their investment in you and pass it along to others.

I think of all those doctors, surgeons, and nurses who put me back together, and they had a smile on their faces every single day. At five o'clock in the morning, they roused me up and announced they were going to put me back together, and I would have a life. I'm so grateful to be surrounded by those people. They were incredible.

My wife is certainly included in that list. We were only engaged for two weeks at the time I was blown up. I'm so thankful I proposed because it was the last time I was able to get on one knee. She left college to be at my side, and she never left. I can't put into words how thankful I am.

My Wife's Perspective

NUMEROUS people have shaped my life, but no one more significantly than my wife, Megan. Not only has she nursed me from the beginning of my rehab in the San Antonio hospital, but she continues to make my life better every day. On top of that, she has given me two sons, the most precious gift anyone can give. With that in mind, I think it's appropriate that you hear from her and gain her perspective on this experience.

Jack and I were good friends in school even though he was two grades ahead of me. In small towns, you know everyone in school, and we always had mutual friends from elementary through high school. I was a sophomore when he was a senior, and he asked me to the senior prom. That was the first time we spent time hanging out with one another. We stayed close, dating off and on as I finished high school. He stayed nearby, going to college to be an electrician. At the same time I was graduating, he enlisted in the military. He left for basic training the same day I moved away to college.

At that point, we said to one another, you do your thing, and I'll do mine, and wished each other luck. I told him to write when he could, but there was no commitment to one another at that time. I remember being off in school, missing our mutual group of friends, and being around his family. I really liked Jack's family and being close to them.

Once he completed basic training, Jack got his phone back, and we started talking. Soon we were talking every day. We were both committed to the relationship at that point. From the time he completed basic, it was only six months before he was deployed. From the moment he enlisted, Jack expected he would be fighting in Afghanistan  one day, so we talked about it a lot. In all the conversations about what that would look like, it was always about whether he might or might not come back. We never gave any thought to him being injured or what life would look like if he were.

I was 18 years old and naïve. I had no idea about how heavy the combat would be where he was going. Once he left, it was common not to hear from him for a couple of weeks at a time. We laughed that we would need to write letters just to communicate. It seems that when we did, they seldom arrived. Sometimes the truck carrying a letter from me to him or from him to me would get blown up. I had no idea what I was getting myself into. I was a small-town girl with a limited worldview.

I worked and went to school. I transferred home from college to be with friends, our mutual group of friends. I wanted to surround myself with people who could support me while Jack was away. Jack and I communicated primarily via Facebook, but the best time for him was three in the morning. I kept the phone near the bed to hear the notification that he was online. We were seldom able to speak. Any communication we had with one another was great but often long in between.

Although I was afraid of what might happen to him, I didn't live in constant fear. It wasn't constantly on my mind. Our communication primarily concerned the mundane things of life. I never wanted him to be in a firefight or something serious and be distracted by a fight with his girlfriend. I struggled with not talking to him frequently, which made it difficult to go anywhere or sleep at night for fear of missing an opportunity.

It was on a Monday or Tuesday morning that I received a call from Jack's mom. The Army contacted his dad about him being wounded since we were not married. He was already on his way to work, so he called Lori as he turned around to return home. She called me, and my phone woke me up at 7:15 in the morning. I remember thinking it was weird that his mom would call me that early.

I had not heard from Jack in a couple of days, and when she called, my heart stopped. I remember answering the phone, saying "hello." I knew right away from the way she was talking there was something wrong. It was obvious she had been crying, and it was so hard for her to talk. I pleaded over and over to tell me if he's alive," just tell me he's alive.," repeatedly. She finally told me that he was alive, but it was really bad.

I called my mom first and said, "Jack got hurt. Lori's coming to get me; it's really bad." I'm sure I was hysterical.

Lori picked me up, and as I got in the car, we were both crying. Our houses were only a mile apart, but it felt like forever. We never said a word, but it wasn't an awkward silence. We were both so scared and sad and had no idea what to say.

I didn't know at that point that he had lost his legs. All I knew was he had been hurt. Jack's dad wasn't there when we got to the house, and she wanted to wait until he got back to tell me. I finally convinced her to tell me what was going on. She tearfully said, "He's alive, but he lost his legs. His legs are gone."

I was leaning against the wall, and I slid down to the floor as she spoke. I pulled my knees up and cried. I remember so many thoughts. "What would his life be like with no legs?" "What prosthetics would he have?" Questions I had no way of answering.

Over the years, many have asked what went through my mind during the five days between getting the information and seeing Jack in San Antonio. I had no idea what the journey would be like, but never once did I think I was not going to be able to do this. The test would be extreme, but there was never a question of whether I wanted to be with him. I was just desperate to get to him. I needed to tell him in person that I still loved him and wanted to be with him. I could not stand the thought of Jack being alone.

Jack had recently been home on leave from Valentine's Day through the end of the month. It was during that time that we got engaged. My birthday is March first, and he returned to Afghanistan days before. He proposed on the last night, so we were only engaged a week before he was wounded.

It's crazy how things work out. I was flying high, dreaming and planning our future, eager to spend my life with him. It felt like nothing could destroy the joy and happiness I was experiencing. When the terrible news arrived, I was ready to dive in and do what was necessary for Jack.

By the time we received the news, he had already been flown to Germany, his first stop on the way to San Antonio. We had no idea if he would be in Germany for hours, days, or weeks, so we started thinking about passports and travel plans. Neither Jack's dad nor I had a passport, but someone in the military contacted the State of Minnesota passport services. We drove to the city and got ours in about ten minutes. If Jack were kept in Germany, we would be able to get to him.

It turned out that he did not stay in Germany, so our plans changed, and we flew to San Antonio. It was the first time in my life to be on an airplane. The military paid for dad, mom, and the oldest sibling but obviously didn't include girlfriends. His brother had just enlisted in the Army and was training in California and couldn't go, so he gave his spot to me. I remember being frantic because my parents weren't well off, and I was a broke college student, but I'm very thankful that I found a way to get to him.

—MEGAN & JACK IN HOSPITAL

It was five days between getting the call about Jack's injury and the day we arrived in San Antonio. The entire time, he was in a medically induced coma. During that time, information about his condition was sparse. They gave us an 800 number we could call every eight hours, and they would provide some information, but it was not like speaking with Jack or anyone near him.

It was nothing more than a brief recap of his medical records.

At one point, we were told one of his arms had been amputated and another time that he was awake and alert, both of which were wrong. The information was all over the place. By the time we arrived, we had no idea about his condition.

When first arriving at the hospital, Jack was in surgery. They directed us to a waiting room. The surgery door opened; we looked up and saw Jack being wheeled down the hallway toward his room. I wasn't prepared to see him. When we were allowed into his room, we had to put on a gown and gloves because he was susceptible to infection. In fact, the entire time he was in the hospital, we wore scrubs caps, yellow gowns, and gloves. Seeing Jack's pale skin was a shock, and it still haunts me.

Being newly engaged, I was not listed on any of Jack's military forms. Even though I ended up being the one at his side taking care of him every day, I was not supposed to be there. I helped with everything that was going on with him, not just in the hospital but also during rehab. I was the one who needed to hear everything that the doctors said and participate in making decisions. I struggled with being heard and accepted as an advocate for Jack. It was awful seeing him in the hospital and everything he went through, but it was nice to have him with me.

We found normal things we could do together. We watched entire series of TV shows while in the hospital. It was a challenge back then because it was the days before available Wi-Fi. I didn't know anyone in San Antonio, and I didn't have a car for getting around town. All I had to do was take care of Jack. When he was in one of those eight to ten-hour surgeries, I was alone and lonely. I struggled to feel a sense of purpose.

Before we had time to take in Jack's condition, they told us that he had drains coming out of his legs, his arms were bandaged, and we would not see the leg amputations because they were covered. They added that he wasn't wearing any clothes and had a ventilator, so he couldn't speak.

I stood in the doorway feeling like I should allow his parents to go in first. They took a position on either side of Jack's bed and just stared at him. It was a heartbreaking sight. This young man who was so tall and strong was now shrunk up in the bed and helpless. He was so fragile that he couldn't survive without someone tending to him constantly.

I latched on to one of the nurses who became a special person to us. Remember, I had nobody in San

Antonio after Jack's parents went home, without even a car for transportation. She proved to be more than a nurse and became a friend. When I needed a haircut, she took me to a hairdresser. She was one of many wonderful people we met in San Antonio.

—JACK AND FIRST TEAM LEADER

We were in ICU for two weeks. Shortly after arriving, they removed the ventilator and Jack was able to speak and communicate. The first time he tried to talk, it scared me to hear the sound of his voice. It was deep and almost sounded desperate. I remember obsessively saying to him, "I'm here, I'm here. I'm not leaving. I'm not going anywhere."

He spoke, almost sounding annoyed, "I hear you, woman. I'm glad to see you too."

I was worried that he might not know who I was. A huge fear went away as soon as he looked at me and said my name. I knew he recognized me. That was something I thought about often—when he wakes up, will he know who I am?

We made it through the hospital ordeal that Jack described earlier, and he was discharged on May twelfth. I remember that date specifically because the night before was when Osama Bin Laden was killed. As you remember, it was all over the news. Although Jack was discharged from the hospital, we stayed in San Antonio for more than a year until October 2012.

Out of the hospital, I quickly realized how unaware people are about the needs of those in a wheelchair. Things as simple as going to a restaurant or is the bathroom door wide enough (it's not always), how high are the tabletops, is there a ramp to get into the building. We had to learn to think in advance before going somewhere.

Jack has always had an amazing attitude when it comes to obstacles. He doesn't worry about what people think. For example, if he comes up to a building with a few steps in front of the door, he climbs out of his chair, makes his way up the stairs, and drags the chair with him to get back in at the top of the steps. He seldom turns away from a challenge. It doesn't bother him, although, I admit, it sometimes bothers me.

I don't want to be put in difficult situations, but he constantly reminds me not to worry about things I can't control; we'll figure it out. Him being the person he is, makes me a better person. It's good for me.

Nobody understands how many obstacles he goes through every day. He's not good at talking about them because his glass is always half full. I try not to be overly cautious, but I understand how hard it is for him to transfer in and out of his chair and do all the other stuff life requires.

Our life together really started when we moved back to Minnesota. We were anxiously waiting to leave and get back to family and friends. As soon as it was possible, we hit the road. Soon we were home and were building a house. I got pregnant, and we were busy seeing everyone and doing all the stuff we missed. Although we had been married a year, it felt like we were starting over.

It has been a very busy ten years. Jack works hard to give back to the community, which is important to both of us. We now have two boys, and they told us we might not be able to have children for a long time. We like to tell William, our oldest, that he was such a wonderful miracle that Benjamin came right after him. I watched Jack work through all the challenges of being a father in a wheelchair, like how do you lay a baby in a crib from the chair, how to change a diaper, how to carry the baby. There were so many adjustments, but that's our life.

Conclusion

I indicated that many of the lessons that have carried me through the past decade were learned, or at least reinforced, during basic training. When I finished, I not only felt like one of the best-trained soldiers on the planet but also that I was equipped to handle numerous other situations in life.

At the conclusion of basic training, they took us on a final field exercise that proved to be unlike any other hike we had experienced. We walked. And we walked until we were at the point that we could walk no further. We walked to a place they called "Stairway to Heaven." It brought us to the gates of the infantry compound. I have no idea of the distance, but I've heard anywhere from 13 to 20 miles. I have no doubts that both could be correct.

After walking all day, carrying who knows how many pounds of equipment on your back, we came to the goal at the end of the path. It felt like everything we had been working toward for the last 13 weeks was close to being achieved. They called it the "Stairway to Heaven," but suddenly we're thinking, where is this stairway?

We walked up a hill and wondered if maybe that was the stairway, but it wasn't. We went a little further, around a corner, and suddenly we could see it. It looked like the highest hill I had ever seen in my entire life. All I could see was level after level, all the way to the top. That's the "Stairway to Heaven," and it's obvious how it got the name.

At that point, we were absolutely smoked, and it was getting dark. After walking all day, everybody was tired and sucking in air. If we were allowed, we would have put our heads down and sat for a rest. But it's not allowed. They come by and scream at you, saying things like, "You're trying to get everybody killed!"

They talked like we were out on a battlefield with the enemy all around. We couldn't stop, or we would die. They did allow a very quick break to get some water and gather our thoughts for a second. One of my buddies said, "I can't go any longer; I can't keep going."

I'll never forget the drill sergeant saying, "You sure you can't take one more step?"

He replied, "I can take one more step."

It was true. All of us could take one more step, no matter how tired we were or impossible the climb ahead of us seemed. We could do one more step.

Here's the key. After you take the one step more, you can then take one more. And then, one more. Soon you realize you can keep going. You have chopped up an impossible task into doable-sized pieces. This realization was one of the most incredible things that changed my life immensely. No matter how far I go, I can always go one step further.

After being wounded in Afghanistan, my first thought was, I can't make it, I can't go any further. There have been so many times in my life that I wanted to give up, but I learned there is always one more step I can take. This realization allowed me to keep my eyes open for five more minutes so the doctor could save my life.

As I went through rehab, this truth stayed with me. Touch my nose one more time. One more pullup. One more pushup. Once more, into the shower.

I strive to approach every challenge with this attitude. When I'm lifting weights in the gym, I tell everyone who sets their own personal record, they have to do it three times. It's not enough to do it just once. Anybody can do one more, so push yourself to do three. If you take one more step, sooner or later, you will make it.

So, we did. We all took one more step. Suddenly, we were walking through the gates of the "Stairway to Heaven," where they had a huge bonfire. They gave us a super-hydrating drink, the best-tasting thing I've ever had. They led us in a ceremony, and we made a giant toast signifying that we had made it, and then we were infantrymen.

From then on, they treated us differently. We were no longer in boot camp. We were infantrymen—real soldiers.